Barcode in Back

1

singkil

singkil
catherine hernandez

playwrights canada press
toronto • canada

Singkil © Copyright 2009 Catherine Hernandez

PLAYWRIGHTS CANADA PRESS
The Canadian Drama Publisher
215 Spadina Ave., Suite 230, Toronto, Ontario, Canada, M5T 2C7
phone 416.703.0013 fax 416.408.3402
orders@playwrightscanada.com • www.playwrightscanada.com

The publisher acknowledges the support of the Canadian taxpayers through
the Government of Canada Book Publishing Industry Development Program,
the Canada Council for the Arts, the Ontario Arts Council, and the Ontario
Media Development Corporation.

 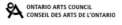

Cover design by Leah Renihan
Cover photo of Catherine Hernandez by Mark McNeilly
Typesetting by Blake Sproule

LIBRARY AND ARCHIVES CANADA CATALOGUING IN PUBLICATION
Hernandez, Catherine, 1977-
Singkil / Catherine Hernandez.

A play.
ISBN 978-0-88754-869-7

I. Title.

PS8615.E75 S55 2009   C812'.6   C2009-900110-1

First edition: February 2009
Printed and bound by Canadian Printco, Scarborough, Ontario, Canada

There are two sounds I will never forget: The sound of my baby's heartbeat and the sound of the Singkil. Thank you to my mother Cecille Estioko Hernandez and my daughter Arden Lani McNeilly for granting me both. Let's keep dancing, shall we?

playwright's note

Even as the umbilical cord is cut between mother and child, the bond remains. No minute goes by in my life where I don't think of the welfare of my own child. Those thirty-nine weeks spent in gestation create this phantom connection between you, even as your son/daughter grows to become a fully grown adult; even beyond the grave.

It was through the realization of this bond that this play was born. Several years ago, I found a photo of my mother, Cecille Hernandez, dancing the ancient dance of the Singkil. There she was, in full traditional costume, re-enacting the legend of a Filipina Muslim princess who braved the terror of an earthquake with grace. Judging by the date on the back of the photo, she was two months pregnant with me. It was a profound moment for me; this idea of me dancing the dance even before my life began; learning the rhythms of my mother.

Singkil is the love child between me and Nina Lee Aquino. Over the course of its four-year gestation, we've both become mothers of beautiful daughters, learned joy and loss, and it speaks, speaks with the volume of an infant cry to each page of this play.

Now it's our turn to cut the cord—and time for you, the reader, to learn the hypnotic rhythms of this beautiful dance. Enjoy.

singkil

catherine hernandez

Singkil was first produced at Factory Theatre as part of their 06/07 season, by fu-GEN Asian-Canadian Theatre Company, in association with Factory Theatre, with the following cast:

MIMI	Nadine Villasin
CHASE	David Yee
MARIA	Karen Ancheta
NESTOR	Leon Aureus
NORMA	Rose Cortez
Director	Nina Lee Aquino
Movement	Clare Preuss
Traditional Choreography	Catherine Hernandez
Sound Design	Romeo Candido
Set Design	Camellia Koo
Lighting Design	Arun Srivinasan
Costume Design	Jackie Chau
Stage Management	Dale Yim
Ass. Stage Management	Eric Chan
Dramaturge	Yvette Nolan
Assoc. Dramaturges	Nina Lee Aquino, Ric Knowles

characters

MIMI	Filipina Canadian, late twenties
CHASE	Mimi's boyfriend, any ethnicity, late twenties
NESTOR	Mimi's father, Filipino, late fifties
MARIA	Mimi's mother, Filipina, early to late fifties
NORMA	Maria's old friend from the Philippines, Filipina, late fifties
MAN	Maria's lover, Caucasian Canadian man, late twenties
TAMMY	Chase's friend, any ethnicity, early twenties

historical background for the singkil

There are many variations on the legend of the Singkil. But this was what was told to me:

> There was a beautiful Maranao princess named Princess Gandingan. While she was walking in the forest, jealous fairies created an earthquake, hoping to kill her with falling bamboo trees and rocks. Much to their chagrin, Princess Gandingan skipped nimbly through the debris. This was later translated into Muslim Filipino folk dance as the Singkil (Maranao word for "getting a leg or foot entangled in an object"), where a solo female performer dances in and out of criss-crossed bamboo poles, keeping time to a hypnotic rhythm, all while waving her fans gracefully.

set

The set is composed of several bamboo poles that can be interchanged to represent different locations.

This play takes place in present-day Scarborough, Ontario, Canada, with flashbacks to Manila, Philippines, and Toronto, Ontario, Canada during the '70s.

act one
scene one

The sound of waves. With each incoming wave, the sound of water intermingles with the sound of metal against metal. A set of headlights is seen in the distance. Screeching tires.

Lights shift to MIMI's apartment at night. There are clothes and boxes everywhere.

MIMI suddenly gets up with a jolt. CHASE lies beside her, grumbling groggily.

MIMI   Shit!

CHASE   What is it?

MIMI   Oh God! I gotta get out of here. What time is it?

CHASE   The time?

MIMI   Yes.

CHASE   I left my cell phone at my place.

MIMI   Where's my watch? I'm sure I'm late.

She starts to leaf through the strewn clothes to find her watch. CHASE starts to help her look, but at a slower pace. She finds her watch. CHASE finds a semi-closed box labelled "MIMI." He picks it up.

Ah-hah! Shit! It's 7:15. I am sooo fucked.

> *She frantically begins to put clothes on and collect her things.*

CHASE   What's the rush?

> *He casually opens the box and takes out a golden Sari Manok headpiece from inside.*

MIMI   I have to pick someone up from the airport.

CHASE   Who?

MIMI   This friend of my mom is coming for a visit.

CHASE   Isn't that a few months too late?

MIMI   I don't get it either.

> *At the sight of him handling the headpiece...*

Whoa! What is that?

CHASE   I dunno.

MIMI   Where did you get that?

CHASE   I just found it in here.

> *He turns it upside down and looks at it.*

MIMI   What are you doing? Put that down!

> *She takes it from him and tries to replace the rather large brass chicken headdress back into the box. She sees her name labelled on the side.*

Jeez!

CHASE   What is it?

MIMI	It's nothing. Just don't touch it.
CHASE	It's a chicken.
MIMI	It was my mom's. She wore it when she danced.
CHASE	She danced?
MIMI	Yes. It's for this dance with poles... and fans and stuff.
CHASE	Whoa! Poles? Are you serious?
MIMI	No, Chase. Not stripper poles. The poles were on the ground. It's a... Filipino thing. It's a thing they do.
CHASE	Was this for her head?
MIMI	Yes! Just... don't touch it. I don't even know what it's doing here.
	She puts the box away and distractedly tries to continue gathering her things for her departure.
CHASE	You don't remember bringing it here?
MIMI	My dad was cleaning out my mom's stuff and... I guess he thought I wanted this.
CHASE	Are you going to give it back, then?
MIMI	I don't know, okay? Maybe we can discuss this when I get back. Just don't touch it.
CHASE	What's with all this stuff I can't touch? Isn't this supposed to be Mimi and Chase's den-o-sin?
MIMI	*(She continues dressing.)* Okay, for your information, this is *my* den-o-sin, not yours.
CHASE	*(jokingly)* Ah! Come on! You're telling me you don't love my

toothbrush taking up that space on your counter? You don't love my lucky sweatshirt draped over your night table?

MIMI   *(seriously)* Love is a strong word.

            She continues to look for her keys while avoiding eye contact.

CHASE   *(through a laugh)* I was... I was joking. Come on. I know love is a strong word, okay? I know I'm only here to open jars of mayo. Fuck. It's not like I go anywhere with you...

MIMI   Are you going to bring this up again?

CHASE   What?

MIMI   My mom's funeral wasn't the ideal place to introduce you to my paren— To my dad.

CHASE   There's nothing wrong with talking, either.

MIMI   Here we go...

CHASE   *(through a laugh)* I mean, what? I find a box with a crown in it. Of course I'm going to look at it. And here you are slapping my wrist like a child. Okay, I get the fucking picture. Don't touch. Am I a suck or something?

MIMI   No! That's not what I'm saying.

            She heads to the washroom. The sound of the tap.

CHASE   Am I too emotional just 'cause I want to know something about you? I didn't even know your mom was a dancer. I don't know much about your parents, period.

            MIMI mumbles something from the washroom.

            What?

Mimi shows herself to Chase, her toothbrush in her mouth.

Ah, never mind.

Mimi quickly spits and re-enters the bedroom.

Mimi   Oh please! For your information, I didn't know much about my mom's years as a dancer, okay?

Chase continues to look away from her.

What? Are you sore now?

Chase   See! You are calling me a suck.

Mimi   No! I was fucking brushing my teeth. Do you want my dad to smell... stuff on me?

Chase   Smell what?

Mimi   You know. *(She begins to giggle.)* Oh God, Chase.

Chase   Smell my manly scent? Smell the marijuana-induced sex we just had?

He grabs her playfully from behind and she shrugs.

Mimi   Chase, I have to go.

Chase tries to unbutton the shirt she just put on.

Look what you're doing to me! I'm in a rush and this is how you help me get out the door?

Chase   Stay for a bit.

Mimi   Hon, I can't.

Pause. Chase wilts.

It's not that I don't want to talk. Seriously. I have to go, all right?

CHASE   Okay.

MIMI   *(kisses him quickly)* Okay.... What was I doing? Oh yeah... my keys. Where the fuck are they?

She continues to search frantically.

CHASE   When are you coming back?

MIMI   I shouldn't be late.

CHASE   Can I eat some of your bread?

MIMI   As long as you don't eat as much as last time. You can have as much peanut butter as you want, but lay off the Nutella, for God's sake. You're eating me out of house and home.

CHASE   Hey, I buy groceries... sometimes.

MIMI   But do you buy the right ice cream?

CHASE   I always buy chocolate fud—

MIMI   See!

CHASE   Chocolate mint! No, I knew it! Fuck. I second-guessed myself. *(pause as he watches her)* I promise to be good.

He twirls her keys playfully on his finger. MIMI reaches to grab them but he holds them beyond her reach.

I love you, you know?

MIMI   I know.

CHASE   I'm here for you.

MIMI   I know.

CHASE   So if you want to…

MIMI   Oh jeez, Chase, I have to go!

CHASE   I know.

MIMI   I'm sorry.

          She kisses him obligingly and grabs the keys from him
          before heading out the door.

act one
scene two

The airport at night. The sound of an airplane punctuates the beginning of the scene. NESTOR and MIMI enter, looking up at the boarding call.

MIMI   Good. It looks like her flight is on time.

NESTOR   *(after much silence)* Thanks for driving, Mimi.

MIMI   Dad... I said forget it. *(pause)* I don't mind driving—really. It's a nice change from taking the TTC. I just wish it was a cooler car.

NESTOR   Why?

MIMI   Well, I'm young, and it's a bit embarrassing driving an Aerostar minivan.

NESTOR   Your cousin Remy drives a minivan. And she's in her twenties.

MIMI   Yeah well, Remy still lets her mom powder her back when she gets sweaty.

NESTOR nods in understanding.

So why didn't this lady make it to the funeral? All of that stuff should have been over and done with a long time ago. What took her so long?

NESTOR   It's harder to afford things there. Now that she'll be here, maybe she can help us clear out your mom's stuff.

MIMI	Speaking of… what's with the box?
NESTOR	The what?

NORMA enters with her luggage in tow. She has obviously taken extra time to freshen up before meeting them.

NORMA	Nestor, my God!

MIMI stays at a distance while NESTOR walks towards NORMA.

NESTOR	Here she is!
MIMI	Oh Jesus.
NESTOR	*Aling,* Norma!
NORMA	You look so old!
NESTOR	And you… after a twenty-nine-hour flight… you smell… so clean.

They share a laugh. They look at each other up and down and smile awkwardly.

NORMA	Bago ito! Maniwala ka, hindi naman ako maka-pigil. Nakita ko to sa duty free doon sa Tokyo—di siempre kailangan bilihin! Di Nama ako puede dumating—pagkatapos ng pagkahaba-habang flight eh di ang bantot-bantot ko na, no? Eh, di siempre na pa bili narin ng pabango at makeup!

NORMA strikes a pose and NESTOR laughs a full-on belly laugh. MIMI looks at him like a stranger. NESTOR nods.

(NORMA looks at him thoughtfully as her tone changes.) Oy si Benny nag hello daw. Si Ging-Ging din. Si Aling Edith nag he-hello din. Naku! Excited silang lahat na napa punta ako dito! *(pause)* I'm glad to finally see you. It has been so long.

She looks at him for a moment, then reaches out and holds NESTOR's hands with an awkward smile.

NESTOR   Yes.

NORMA   *(tentatively)* How are you doing?

MIMI coughs indicatively. NESTOR quickly gestures to MIMI and NORMA looks in her direction.

And who is this?

NESTOR   This is—

MIMI   Hi, I'm Mimi.

She extends her hand in a businesslike manner.

NORMA   You look... so much like your mommy! Give *Ate* Norma a hug.

MIMI   *(They hug.)* Welcome to Canada, *Tita* Norma.

NORMA   Oh-oh-oh, it's *Ate* Norma. Do I look old enough to be an aunt?

MIMI   Okay, *Ate* Norma.

NORMA   I can't tell you how excited I am to finally be here. *(pause)* So this is *the* Pearson Airport?

MIMI   Yes.

NORMA   And is that...

MIMI   Snow.

NORMA   Uh-huh.

She stares out the windows.

NESTOR   Let's go now, there's much more to Toronto than the Pearson Airport. I have lots of food ready at home.

> *NORMA suddenly stops and looks at them and out the windows, not knowing what to say. NESTOR kindly removes his own jacket and places it over NORMA's shoulders. NORMA is positively elated as she and NESTOR exit.*
>
> *MIMI trails behind.*

act one
scene three

*The airport, 1974. The sound of an airplane punctuates
the beginning of the scene. The sound of '70s elevator
music is heard. The morning light is dawning.*

*Maria, Mimi's late mother, comes in with her huge
luggage. She throws her luggage down in a huff and sits
on it. She begins to cry. Nestor enters wearing a leather
jacket of the period and approaches Maria.*

NESTOR   *(à la "American" accent)* Do you come here often?

MARIA   *(gets up with a jolt)* Nestor! Oh my God. *(They embrace. She
          pauses and looks him up and down)* You're... so... fat.

          She resumes her crying while embracing him.

NESTOR   Darling.... What's wrong?

MARIA   *(frantically, without taking a breath)* Nestor... I can't believe
          I'm finally here. I... I sat in that airplane for more than a day,
          I kept looking out the window and all I saw was water and
          more water, I would fall asleep and when I awoke I wasn't
          sure what time it was, when was I supposed to eat? When was
          I supposed to sleep? The morning looked like the afternoon,
          the night looked like the morning and I felt so lost and the kid
          in the seat in front of me peed on my luggage...

NESTOR   Ohhhh— I love you—

MARIA   *(just as he is about to kiss her tenderly)* When the plane landed
          everyone clapped so loudly, like we were crazy. We were
          in there for so long we all wanted to get out as quickly as

possible, all of us had been sitting for so long, looking out the window, and when I came out of the gate you weren't here! I thought I was in the wrong city.

NESTOR   No, you're in the right place. Welcome to Toronto... *Mrs. Perez.*

MARIA   *(She smiles.)* Stop. *(She eyes him up and down.)* How did you get so fat? You've only been here for a couple of months.

NESTOR   What do you mean? This is a handsome figure!

MARIA   *Gago!*

NESTOR   Everyone here eats hamburgers. Look around, everyone else is fat here.

She looks around and out the windows.

MARIA   My God.

NESTOR   What is it?

MARIA   It's sunny.

NESTOR   It's July.

MARIA   There's no snow. *Aling* Norma's cousin saw snow when she came to Canada.

NESTOR   Not now, darling. It will come soon. *(He touches MARIA's face.)* I love you.

> *Lights change. Manila, 1972. They are standing millimetres apart, face to face, as they deliver the following text. NESTOR's touch to MARIA's face is suddenly drawn away in bashfulness.*

MARIA   What did you say?

NESTOR	I said...
MARIA	Yes?
NESTOR	I said, I love you.
MARIA	You what?
NESTOR	I love you. *(pause)* Yes. It's true. *(pause)* I love you, I love you, I think about you every night and every day. I think about the kids we will have and how I will take care of you some day I love you Maria I love you I love you I love you I can't help but smile when I look at you I don't know why this is happening to me I can't stop talking I can hardly breathe I love you I love you I love you...
MARIA	I love you too!

They embrace tightly.

NESTOR	You do?! Because I love you, Maria...
MARIA	Yes! Yes, I know!

They embrace once more. Lights change. Pearson Airport, 1974. MARIA suddenly looks at NESTOR, fearful. The sound of a lullaby gone wrong is heard.

Nestor, I'm scared.

NESTOR	Of what?
MARIA	Of everything being so new.
NESTOR	Manila has changed, Maria. We have to change too.

He grabs the luggage and begins to walk. MARIA watches him as he walks ahead of her.

MARIA	Nestor?

NESTOR   *(He stops.)* Yes?

MARIA   *(She thinks for a second, then changes her mind)* I'm hungry.

> *Lights change and* MARIA *is pushed into the ground.* NESTOR *watches as a fast and furious procession begins to bury her deep in a forest of bamboo, just as fast as a door slamming. The sound of throat singing.* MARIA *steps into the coffin, a procession closes the casket and she is spirited off.* NESTOR *remains neutral, but begins to join in on the throat singing. A series of well-wishers enter, placing a hand on* NESTOR's *shoulders and walking away, leaving him in a spotlight.*

PROCESSION *(whispering, as touching him on the shoulders)* Sorry about the loss. Sorry about. Sorry loss. Sorry. Sorry. Sorry. Sorry. Sorry. Sorry. Sorry.

> *The throat singing builds to a climax,* NESTOR *is about to scream...*

Rose Cortez, David Yee, Leon Aureus, and Nadine Villasin
photo by Mark McNeilly

17

act one
scene four

The Perez house at night. MIMI enters suddenly, snapping NESTOR out of his daydream. NORMA can be heard offstage, singing.

MIMI   Dad!

NESTOR   Ha?

MIMI   Dad... did you hear me?

NESTOR   What is it, *anak*?

MIMI   *(whispers)* Who-is-this-lady?

NESTOR   I told you... your *Tita* Norma.

MIMI   I know that, Dad. But... didn't you see the way she... don't you find her... strange? Is she, like, family or something?

NESTOR   Of course.

The sound of muffled singing.

MIMI   No, that's not what I meant. Is she, like, related to us?

NESTOR   No, we were friends back home.

MIMI   I just find her weird... with you. Do you not see this? Am I the only one who—

The singing is broken up with static. Both MIMI and NESTOR stop in their tracks and look at one another.

18

NORMA   *(from offstage) Ano ito?* Check. Checking. Checking.

MIMI   What is she doing?

           They walk to stage right to find NORMA *with a toy
           karaoke mic in hand, its speaker working intermittently.
           NORMA sees NESTOR and MIMI looking at her.*

NORMA   Ay! I got this too at the duty free. It was on sale. *(The batteries
           come undone and she clumsily puts it away)* Anyways... I'll put
           this away for now. It's *pasalubong* time.

MIMI   Pasa-what?

NORMA   I have presents for you. Here. Catch!

           She throws MIMI *a bag labelled "Shoe Mart."*

MIMI   What is this?

NORMA   It's a gift.

MIMI   You shouldn't have...

NORMA   I know.

MIMI   I can't...

NORMA   Just open it already.

           *MIMI opens the package and finds a plethora of cotton
           undies in a vast array of Easter-egg-like colours.*

MIMI   Wow.

NESTOR   Say thank you to your *Ate* Norma.

MIMI   These are... really big panties. And these... *(She pulls out a
           tangle of firm-shaped bras in size A.)* are really small bras.

19

NESTOR	Mimi...
NORMA	And look at this. It's for you. *(She gives MIMI a navy blue drawstring bag with a toothbrush in it.)* I got this from Philippine Airlines. Look at it.
MIMI	It's a toothbrush.
NORMA	No, look at it. See? You unscrew this end and there's the toothpaste. A toothbrush and toothpaste, all in one.
MIMI	*(sarcastically)* I will cherish—
NESTOR	That is very generous, Norma.
NORMA	*(to NESTOR)* And for you. *(She presents him with a pen. NESTOR bashfully takes it.)* I had it custom-made... since you are left-handed... and it has your name... engraved... right here... *(She runs to her bag and gives him a pile of stationery.)* Oh ito... stationery para maka sulat ka... kahit ka nino. Diba?
NESTOR	You remembered... I'm left-handed.
NORMA	Siempre naman! Naalalamo ba noong na lalaro tayo ng Pasoy Dos?
	NESTOR nods, blushing.
	Lagi kong na pa pansin na kaliwete ang pag hawak mo ng cards.
MIMI	*(stiffly interrupting them)* Wow. This is very generous of you. Panties, bras, pens.
NORMA	*(still looking at NESTOR)* No problem! They were on sale at Shoe Mart. I even got some for myself.
MIMI	You mean Wal-Mart.
NORMA	No, not Wal-Mart. Shoe Mart.

MIMI	Shoe what?
NORMA	The mall in the Philippines.
MIMI	An entire mall devoted to shoes?
NORMA	No, there's lots of panties there, too. Nestor, has she never been back home?
NESTOR	No, she hasn't.
NORMA	Ay, my God! You don't know what you're missing if you've never been back home.
MIMI	We just never went.
NORMA	*(pause)* Your mommy would be very proud if you decided to go, you know.
MIMI	Why would you say that?
NORMA	She was very proud of her home country.
MIMI	Did she tell you that?
NORMA	*(Pause. NORMA looks to NESTOR.)* She did... before. Why?
MIMI	She didn't talk about it much.
NORMA	Oh.
MIMI	And I never heard about you until I heard you were coming.
NORMA	*(looking to NESTOR)* No?

> *NESTOR avoids eye contact and goes to the kitchen to pack MIMI's leftovers.*

We were dancers together.

MIMI	*(looking to NESTOR)* Oh really?
NORMA	When she moved to Canada, I continued dancing in the Philippines and she started her family.
MIMI	*(pause)* And here I am.
NORMA	*(pause)* Your mom was a beautiful dancer.
MIMI	I heard. *(looks at NESTOR pointedly)* It looks like I have her headdress now. Right, Dad?
NORMA	Her Sari Manok? You know, your mommy wore that headdress with such pride.
MIMI	*(sarcastically, sharing a look with her father)* Yeah, Dad. It was very nice of you to give it to me.
NESTOR	You have the Sari Manok?
MIMI	Why did you do that? What were you thinking? What would I do with that headdress?
NESTOR	Where was it?
MIMI	In my apartment, Dad. Where you left it. You think I wouldn't find a box in my own apartment?
NESTOR	I didn't leave it there.
MIMI	Come on now. Don't play dumb.
NESTOR	I didn't even know where it was.
MIMI	Okay. Whatever you say, Dad. It just magically appeared in my apartment. Whatever.
NORMA	Maybe your mom put it there.

NORMA laughs nonchalantly at the thought, her giggles piercing the silence from NESTOR and MIMI.

MIMI   That is the stupidest thing I've ever heard.

NESTOR   Mimi—

NORMA   *Anak,* maybe your mom wants you to have it, so that you can dance the Singkil.

MIMI   What are you talking about?

NORMA   The dance your mommy used to do.

MIMI   Stop.

NORMA   But I think—

MIMI   Stop!

           Pause.

NESTOR   Mimi, anak, gusto mo ng kape? Gawan kita ng kape, ha? Halika, samahan mo ako sa kusina—

MIMI   Not now, Dad.

NORMA   When your mommy danced the Singkil... she was a true princess.

NESTOR   Norma? Coffee?

MIMI   Not now, Dad. *(to NORMA)* Yeah. A true princess. I bet she was.

NORMA   I'm sure she would want you to learn.

MIMI   *(through a mock laugh)* I doubt that. She was a horrible teacher. Mom never taught me. I saw pictures of her. That was about it.

There was a lot she kept from us. *(shifting uncomfortably)* Sorry *Ate... Tita...* whatever.

> *Mimi suddenly gets up and faces away from them for a brief moment. She is pinching her lip.*

NESTOR   *Anak?* *(to Norma)* This is a hard time—

MIMI   No, Dad, there's just something in my—

NESTOR   Sometimes when we think about—

MIMI   Dad, not now.

NORMA   No, no. It's okay. It's hard.

MIMI   *(curtly, turning around again, her face like stone)* Yeah it is. This is all very weird, you know?

NORMA   Yes, of course.

MIMI   It's a bad time to have guests right now. It's a bad time, period. Well, you know what has just happened to us. It's very easy to get sick of people being around while we're going through all this. And I hardly even know you.

NORMA   Yes, yes.

MIMI   And this is just a point of contention between me and my dad.

NESTOR   Mimi...

MIMI   It's just... it seems my mother wasn't very talkative.

NESTOR   Mimi...

MIMI   Particularly to me.

NESTOR   Mimi, that's not true.

NORMA   Oh.

MIMI   It is true, Dad. At least it *was*.

NESTOR   Mimi...

MIMI   She's dead now. *(Silence all around. To NORMA.)* Sorry, I don't
           even know you. I don't know why I'm saying this in front of
           you. This is just a bad time right now.

NORMA   *(pause)* I could teach you the Singkil.

MIMI   What? *(pause)* Wow. This is getting stranger every minute. I
           really can't talk about this right now. That's not what this is
           about.

NORMA   I'm not doing——

MIMI   I know what you're doing. Or *trying* to do. Everyone who has
           stepped through that door over the last few months has been
           trying to do *something*. It would have been fucking awesome
           if you *tried* to see your "friend" a long time ago when she was
           trying to get out of our lives! *(pause)* And by the way, I'm not
           a dancer.

NORMA   It *is* possible. You've been dancing the Singkil your entire
           life.

MIMI   Is that so? *(pause)* Look, I've got to go.

NESTOR   I'm still packing your leftovers, Mimi.

MIMI   Not now, Dad. I don't need it. I have to go.

NESTOR   But it's almost ready.

MIMI   Not now, Dad!

NESTOR   It'll just take a second...

> *NESTOR goes quickly between them with an open Tupperware container and doesn't see a chair two feet in front of him. The container smashes to the floor.*

Ay, shit. I'm sorry.

NORMA   I'll help you clean up.

MIMI   *(at the mess)* Not again. Dad, couldn't you— I have to go.

NESTOR   Mimi, please.

NORMA   Aren't you going to help your father clean up?

MIMI   No. I have to go. Bye, *Tita* Norma. Thanks for the gift.

> *She exits.*

NORMA   *(calling after her) Ate* Norma. It's *Ate* Norma.

> *MIMI exits in a huff. As she leaves the house, the lights change. The sound of an eerie chant is heard, vaguely sounding like the words "Where are you?" in Tagalog. MIMI looks around her, wary and shaken.*

MIMI   Who's there?

> *She continues to exit, cautiously looking behind her.*

act one
scene five

Mimi walks furiously into the darkness. Piercing the black are two headlights, seen in the distance. A cab in Scarborough—at night. It slows down and pulls up next to her.

CABBIE   Need a ride, miss?

MIMI   I'm all right. *(She looks at a bus shelter ahead, alone and desolate.)* Actually... never mind. Sure.

She gets inside.

CABBIE   Where to?

MIMI   McCowan and Sheppard, please.

CABBIE   You're lucky you found me.

MIMI   Why's that?

CABBIE   You just never know who or what's gonna getcha on a night like this.

MIMI   What's wrong with tonight?

CABBIE   It's just one of those nights.

MIMI   Wait! You didn't start your meter.

CABBIE   Doesn't matter.

MIMI   You have to start it, or else it's a free ride.

CABBIE   It's never a free ride. Everything comes at a cost, Mimi.

           Whispers from offstage: "Mimi! Mimi!"

MIMI   What? How did you know my... I want to get off here, please.

CABBIE   This isn't your stop, Mimi. You're not listening.

MIMI   Let me out!

           The CABBIE turns and it's MARIA. MIMI screams.

CABBIE/MARIA   Here's your change, Mimi.

           The cabbie drops shattered pieces of a Sari Manok in MIMI's lap.

MIMI   AHHHH!

CABBIE/MARIA   Why did you break it?

           Whispers from offstage: "Why did you break it? Why did you break it?"

           Lights change. MIMI's apartment.

           MIMI gets up from her bed with a jolt, CHASE is startled beside her.

MIMI   It's broken!

CHASE   What is it?

           Lights up on the box labelled MIMI. MIMI hesitantly approaches the box, knowing something is amiss.

MIMI   *(She opens it and finds the headdress upside down.)* Ahhhhh!

CHASE   What's wrong?

MIMI	It's broken! Didn't I tell you not to touch this?
CHASE	I didn't.
MIMI	Then why is this packed upside down?
CHASE	Because you packed it upside—
MIMI	No I didn't! *(She stops herself.)* Nevermind.
CHASE	Why? Is it okay?
MIMI	*(She looks at the Sari Manok and sees it has a bent beak.)* Shit! The beak is broken!
CHASE	Let me look... it's not broken, sweetie.
MIMI	No! I mean... sorry. I just... I didn't even want this and I've... fucking broken it!
CHASE	Sweetie, the beak is just bent. I'm sure I can fix this...
MIMI	I don't know.
CHASE	Hey.... Are you okay?
	MIMI's lip trembles.
MIMI	Excuse me. I need to—
	Before CHASE says anything, she rushes to the washroom and shuts the door. She covers her mouth as she sobs for a brief second. She goes to the sink and washes her face and looks at her reflection.
	The sound of the chant is heard again, but this time, it is infused with the whispered word, "Push!"

act one
scene six

Toronto, 1975. The chant continues as Maria's *voice is added to the mix. She is moaning in labour. She is drenched in sweat, is on her knees with arms held upwards, looking at a dim light downstage, as though she is being tortured.*

Maria Ooooohhhh. I... I... pleasepleasepleaseplease. Ooooooooh.

Whispers are heard through the chanting. The cast enters as though hunting a wild boar, Maria *their target. They place bamboo about her like a cage and begin to push her in all directions.*

Whisperer Push! Push!

Maria I... I... oooohhhh.... Ahhhh!

Whisperer Touch the head of your baby.

Maria hesitates but then touches her crotch.

Maria Oh God... oh please...

Whisperer It's coming... it's coming!

Maria lets out this moan of release. The chanting stops abruptly. Silence. She is positively shaken. She looks up at the light.

Maria?

Maria flinches.

Maria? Would you like to hold her?

MARIA   *(She weakly holds out her arms to take the baby.)* It's a girl?

WHISPERER Yes.

       Light changes.

MARIA   The nurse hands me my daughter. She feels warm and soft like my insides. She moves towards my breast and begins to suck. I shudder. I shudder. Please don't touch me. I see Nestor about to ceremoniously cut the umbilical cord. I think, "No! Please don't. Please don't unleash her. Please don't let her..."

The nurse asks me if I'm all right.

Am I all right? I don't... why am I not crying in happiness? I don't want to hold her. I don't want her near me. She won't stop crying...

       The lights change to show the sun rising and setting at a fast pace.

Yes, I'm all right. Yes, I love being a mother. Yes, I love my daughter. Of course I love my daughter. Everything's okay. I'm okay. She wakes, I feed her. I put her to sleep. She wakes, I feed her. I put her to sleep. She wakes, I feed her. I put her to sleep.

Stop crying! Oh God, why won't she stop? You want to kill me. My baby wants to kill me. Please stop crying. Please stop crying. Please. Please. Please!

I smile. I notice everyone watching me. They know something is wrong. They keep on asking me if they can help, but the answer is always the same. I don't know. I don't know. If I knew, I would have done it myself. I can't shake this feeling. I can't stop sinking lower into this grey cloud.

       The phone rings and MARIA is startled. The light changes.

The voice of a surveyor is heard.

Hello?

SURVEYOR   Hello there. May I speak to Mr. or Mrs. Pears, please.

MARIA   I am Mrs. Perez.

SURVEYOR   I'm calling from Manley Marketing. Do you have ten minutes to spare?

MARIA   Okay.

SURVEYOR   *(surprised)* Oh! Fantastic. Well, first we must determine if you qualify. Do you mind if I ask you a few questions?

MARIA   No.

SURVEYOR   All right. First off, what age are you?

MARIA   Twenty-six.

SURVEYOR   Oh good! Twenty-six is actually our cut-off age.

MARIA   That's close.

SURVEYOR   I know! Pretty lucky, eh? Okay, what was your highest level of education?

MARIA   I... I went to Santa Clara Parish School.

SURVEYOR   And that was?

MARIA   A high school.

SURVEYOR   And you graduated in what year?

MARIA   I... did not.

SURVEYOR   Oh...

MARIA   I became a dancer.

SURVEYOR Wow.

MARIA   I began touring at a very young age, so of course, I couldn't
          go to school.

SURVEYOR That must have been interesting...

MARIA   It was... it was wonderful.

SURVEYOR But I'm afraid you don't qualify for this study, Mrs. Pears.

MARIA   No?

SURVEYOR Nope. Unfortunately this is specifically for university
          graduates. We're following education course study and career
          placement.

MARIA   Oh. *(There is a long pause.)* You can't ask me any questions?

SURVEYOR No, I can't, Mrs. Pears. Sorry.

MARIA   Oh.

          *The rest of the cast enters with four bamboo poles,
          humming a traditional Muslim Filipino song as the lights
          change. MARIA watches the procession enter, entranced.*

SURVEYOR Are you still there?

MARIA   Have you ever spoken to a princess?

          *They place the bamboo poles in front of MARIA in a
          criss-crossed fashion. The sound of bamboo clapping
          punctuates the air, beating in a steady, Singkil rhythm.
          Boom, boom, boom, clap, clap.*

SURVEYOR Hello? Mrs. Pears? Are you all right?

MARIA   Thirty-three cities.

SURVEYOR   Hello?

MARIA   Thirty-three cities. A different audience every time, but the
             story was always the same.

> *MARIA drops the phone as her slave* Asik *girl enters,
> umbrella in hand, as a lady in waiting for MARIA. She
> ceremoniously presents MARIA with fans. Slowly MARIA
> takes them and begins a seductive fan-play, accompanied
> by the delicate roll of a Kulintang. With grace, she begins
> to step in and out of the criss-crossed bamboo in time
> with the rhythm. Much like a Baptist minister's sermon,
> the rhythm begins to put her into a trance, and she
> becomes delirious with nostalgia while telling the story.
> She uses her fans to illustrate the story and begins to
> dance with the grace of a princess.*

There once lived the beautiful Princess Gandigan on the
island of Mindinao. One day, while strolling through a forest
with her slave, she encountered the fluttering wings of the
Diwata fairies.

Who dares to walk through our enchanted forest?

Why, it is me, daughter to the sultan! The princess's arrogance
insulted the fairies so much that they made the forest rumble
with an earthquake. All of the palm trees were uprooted and
fell at the princess's feet.

> *The rhythm's pace is quickened.*

She looked to her left. She looked to her right. *(The* Asik *girl
dances with arms outstretched.)* Her slave was just beyond
arm's reach. She had no one to turn to. No one but herself.

From deep within her, she gathered all the strength within
her heart to keep her head held high.

Let the trees fall! Let the earth shake! I will prevail!

She nimbly walked through the debris with the grace of her lineage. And with one stroke of her fan, the earth became suddenly silent.

The bamboo clapping rises to a climax and ends abruptly. The lighting changes. MARIA is out of breath.

Then she had a baby and lived happily ever after.

The bamboo claps one last time. A pair of headlights are seen in the distance, a car drives towards her. MARIA shields herself from the brightness of the lights.

Rose Cortez and Nadine Villasin, photo by Mark McNeilly

act one
scene seven

The lights change. The Asik *girl reveals herself under her umbrella and it is* Norma.

NORMA   Dear Maria, congratulations on your new baby girl. I heard from your parents that she is doing well. Thank the Lord. I wish you the best. I... I wish I could see her. And you. And Nestor. It is wonderful that Nestor already has work.

Lights up on Nestor *with a hard hat on, looking at blueprints. Futuristic '70s music is heard.*

NESTOR   The CN Tower is the way of the future. More than 7,000 cubic metres of concrete will go into building the tallest free-standing tower in the world... and I will be part of creating it.

NORMA   Dear Maria, The dance company is doing well and we are scheduled to tour Japan next fall.

NESTOR   I shake hands with great men. Smart men. Wealthy men.

NORMA   I want to know how you are doing. I haven't heard from you, and your parents tell me you hardly call them.

NESTOR   I just smile and do my menial job. Pressing buttons and hammering nails.

NORMA   Why have you not written me? I miss you. I think about you often. I wonder how you are. Things haven't been the same here. We are struggling to get by.

NESTOR   I never have the courage to tell anyone I graduated from the University of Santo Tomas, College of Architecture.

NORMA   Dear Maria, I write you this letter. I write every word knowing you will never read it.

NESTOR   At 9:52 a.m. March 1, 1975, the final piece of the CN Tower is put into place and my job is done. I come home to tell Maria the news, but I find her sleeping with the baby beside her. I go to bed in complete silence.

act one
scene eight

Lights change. A bubble-tea house. TAMMY sits inside, and at the sight of CHASE and MIMI, waves.

TAMMY   Over here!

MIMI stops in her tracks and looks at CHASE.

MIMI   Who is that?

CHASE   Tammy. I told you.

MIMI   I thought you said Timmy.

CHASE   Do I look like someone who hangs out with a Timmy?

MIMI   So you hang out with her?

TAMMY   *(from a distance)* Hi there. You must be Mimi. So nice to meet you finally. I've heard so much about you.

MIMI   Hi. Tammy.

TAMMY   And how are you? *(TAMMY and CHASE kiss each other on the cheeks and sit down. MIMI watches closely.)* I saved you both a seat. *(TAMMY looks under her bum and gets up.)* Wait, stop.

MIMI   What?

TAMMY   Let's trade chairs. Mine is the only one with padding. You take it.

MIMI   No, it's okay.

TAMMY	I insist. I can take your rattan chair.

Mimi takes the seat.

MIMI	Wow, it's still warm.
TAMMY	Anything for Chase's girl. I am such a big fan of his.
CHASE	Stop.
TAMMY	Chase is so talented. Did you ever read that article he wrote on that anorexia clinic?
MIMI	Sure.

Lights change. Chapters bookstore. CHASE is seated behind a table. A stack of books beside him.

Hi—

CHASE	The washroom is over there.
MIMI	No... I.... Are you? *(She holds up her copy of his book.)*
CHASE	Oh! Yes. Yes, I am. Hi, I'm Chase.
MIMI	Hi. Mimi.
CHASE	Thank God. I didn't think anyone read my book.
MIMI	I... I didn't.
CHASE	What?
MIMI	I haven't read the book *yet*, but...
CHASE	Oh.
MIMI	But I've read your article.

CHASE	Which one?
MIMI	Which? The one that was out recently. The one at that anorexia clinic. I just loved it.
CHASE	Oh yes! Boy, did I get skinny.
MIMI	*(laughing)* I loved it. It was very funny.
CHASE	Thanks.
MIMI	So I bought your book in case it was just as funny.

They look at each other.

CHASE	Well, here. Do you want me to sign it? Would you like twenty copies with my signature in it?
MIMI	Sure!

He takes out his pen and begins to write.

CHASE	Fuck. The fucking pen doesn't work.

MIMI laughs.

Don't just stand there laughing. Do you have a pen?

MIMI	No.

MIMI laughs harder. She pauses to find CHASE staring at her. Pause.

CHASE	Jeez. You know what? It has been one long day. Do you want to head over to Starbucks for a coffee? We just have to go... well... it's beside us. And we can listen to Putamayo music while we talk. They may even have a pen. *(He laughs. Sees MIMI looking at him.)* Or... maybe not. Whatever you want to do. *(pause)* Is there something on my face?

MIMI	No! Sorry, I was just… never mind.
CHASE	Do you want to…
MIMI	Sure, let's go.

Lights change. The bubble-tea house.

What kind of place is this?

TAMMY	Oh, you know, it's kind of like Shanghai Pop, Harijuku-girls type stuff. So what kind of bubble tea can I get you, Mimi?
MIMI	None thanks. Tapioca pearls give me gas.
CHASE	You don't see that stopping me. *Garçon!*

CHASE mockingly snaps his finger. TAMMY laughs. MIMI looks at him like a stranger.

What?

MIMI	Nothing.
TAMMY	I'm so sorry. I had no idea you had a tapioca-pearl sensitivity. I would have gotten us a table over at Dooney's or something.
MIMI	It's okay.
TAMMY	You know what, though? They do have an excellent bubble tea with barley instead of tapioca pearls.
MIMI	No, really, I'm okay.
TAMMY	Or you can order whatever you like and I can take the tapioca pearls out.
MIMI	Umm… no thank you.
TAMMY	All right then. *(pause)* So what do you do, Mimi?

MIMI	Nothing. I just work. You know.
CHASE	You don't just work.
MIMI	What?
CHASE	Really, Mimi is good at everything she does.
MIMI	Okay.
CHASE	Come on. Tell her how you streamlined that website thing with that big company. What was the company?
MIMI	I don't remember.
CHASE	You and Tammy have a lot in common.
TAMMY	I'm the webmaster for Single Solutions. But Chase here is what I want to be. Mr. Writer Supreme.
MIMI	Wow.
TAMMY	No, seriously. I love his work.
CHASE	No you don't.
TAMMY	I've read most of your work, right, Chase?
CHASE	There's not much to speak of.
TAMMY	I'm a wannabe writer, too, as Chase knows.
MIMI	Cool.
TAMMY	He has been so helpful with the latest draft of my narrative story. In the course I'm taking, we had to incorporate the elements of earth, fire, and water, and I was seriously stuck. And when I asked for his help, his suggestions just brought it all to life.

CHASE   I don't know.

TAMMY   I mean, I've never even been to India, but setting it up in
            Bombay worked so well.

CHASE   You didn't need much help at all. You have a talent for
            storytelling.

            *MIMI begins to laugh, first to herself, then loud enough to
            get everyone's attention.*

TAMMY   What?

MIMI   I'm sorry. You've never been to India?

TAMMY   No.

MIMI   But you're writing about... *(She laughs.)* Okay. Sorry. *(She
            laughs even more.)*

CHASE   *(intervening)* Have you ever been to India?

MIMI   No. I haven't. I haven't had any time.

CHASE   Sure.

MIMI   *(under her breath)* What the fuck are you doing?

            *A waitress (MARIA) enters with a tray full of bubble-tea
            glasses.*

TAMMY   Here's the waitress. Mimi, are you sure you don't want to try
            something?

            *MIMI is too bothered by the waitress/MARIA. The waitress
            moves stealthily as she places the glasses onto the table.*

            Mimi, are you all right? Mimi? Listen, Chase has told me
            about your mom and everything—

CHASE   Tammy—

TAMMY   And I just wanted to tell you that you can come to me anytime.
           Seriously. Here, I'll give you my card.

MIMI   *(She tosses the card aside.)* I can't fucking believe this. *(MIMI
           stumbles trying to get out of her seat. CHASE follows her.)*

CHASE   What's wrong now?

MIMI   What's wrong? Why the fuck did you bring me here?

CHASE   I wanted to be with you.

MIMI   To be with me? *(gesturing towards TAMMY.)* Or her?

CHASE   That's stupid.

MIMI   No, you know what's stupid? Telling her about my mom.

CHASE   I just stated a fact. I never went into details. She was just
           offering—

MIMI   That is not the point.

CHASE   What is the fucking point, Mimi? What is the point in us ever
           talking? You never want to do it.

MIMI   I'm going home.

           MIMI heads for the exit.

           The lights momentarily change, everything falls silent.

CHASE   Your mom says she's not fooling around anymore. She needs
           to talk.

           MIMI freezes in her tracks.

The lights change back, sound resumes. MIMI *looks at* CHASE, *horrified.*

MIMI   What did you say?

CHASE   I said, this isn't fun anymore. We need to talk.

MIMI thinks for a second, then leaves.

act one
scene nine

*The sound of the car is succeeded by the falling bamboo
in a tangled lattice. NORMA and NESTOR enter at opposite
ends of the stage, slowly moving towards one another. A
steady drum beat is heard. NORMA is pursuing NESTOR,
NESTOR is blindly moving about the bamboo.*

NORMA   I will take his hand.

NESTOR   Two steps. Turn right. The door to the kitchen.

NORMA   And when he looks at me, I will look back.

NESTOR   Fourth button on the left is the broiler.

NORMA   I will ask him. I will tell him everything I want to say.

NESTOR   The cupboard above the microwave, second shelf.

NORMA   He must know. He must.

NESTOR   The colours, the shadows.

NORMA/NESTOR   I cannot make a mistake.

>   *Just as NORMA is about to make contact with NESTOR,
>   MARIA enters. Lights change.*
>
>   *Flashback to a wedding. Soft, slow rumba music is heard.
>   Couples enter the dance floor and begin to slow dance.*

MARIA   Nestor?

NESTOR	Yes?
MARIA	Where were you?
NESTOR	Taking pictures of the bride and groom.

They watch everyone dance.

MARIA	They look very happy.
NESTOR	I think so. You look beautiful. *(He looks at the couples dancing.)* I'm sure you want to dance...
MARIA	Do you want to?
NESTOR	I'm no Fred Astaire.
MARIA	I know you aren't.

They go to the dance floor and begin dancing.

NESTOR	Here is good.
MARIA	I can't... where is your hand? I can't even see your hand.
NESTOR	Sorry... here it is.
MARIA	There, see? You're doing well.
NESTOR	I feel so clumsy.
MARIA	You're not.
NESTOR	It's strange. It's so dark in here, I can barely see your face.

They both move in for an awkward kiss. They continue to dance, and MARIA looks at NESTOR.

What's wrong?

MARIA	I'm holding you. I know it's you. But you feel like a stranger.
NESTOR	Move this way into the light. Can you see me now?
MARIA	Barely.

Lights change. The music changes to a quick cha-cha. NESTOR stops.

NESTOR	This is silly. I don't even know this dance.
MARIA	It's not. We can do this.
NESTOR	I look silly.
MARIA	You look great. Just keep up.
NESTOR	I think I'm going to— *(He steps on MARIA's foot.)* Sorry! I didn't see your foot—
MARIA	Ay!
NESTOR	I should call to see if Mimi's all right.

He begins to exit stage left.

MARIA	She's fine.
NESTOR	Just in case…
MARIA	Dance with me.
NESTOR	I'll be right back.
MARIA	Nestor…
NESTOR	*(He looks back and smiles.)* She's our little princess.

He exits.

The soft, slow rumba is heard again, and a man enters and asks MARIA for a dance. She looks in NESTOR's direction and accepts. The dance becomes hypnotic and grinding. The man moves to exit, and then looks in MARIA's direction before gesturing for her to follow him.

They exit.

act one
scene ten

The Perez house. MIMI enters with box in hand. NORMA enters wearing rubber gloves and carrying several bags and cleaning implements.

MIMI   I need to talk to my dad.

NORMA   He's taking a nap. What is it?

MIMI   *(indicating the box)* I have to give this back to him.

NORMA   Why?

MIMI   It's not mine. And plus... *(She shows her the beak.)* I... I'm sorry, but it's broken, and I think Dad can fix it.

NORMA   Let me take a look.

          She puts down her parcels and looks at the beak closely. She bends it back together.

MIMI   *(reaching to touch it)* Oh good...

NORMA   No, not yet!

          She reaches into her cleaning supplies and pulls out a paper towel and polishes it. MIMI watches her. MIMI reaches her hands out to the Sari Manok.

          Just a sec! Just a sec!

          NORMA tightens the chain links and polishes it even more. MIMI watches her. NORMA looks at MIMI for a moment, then presents the headdress back to MIMI.

Ta-dah!

MIMI   Thanks. *(pause)* Thanks a lot.

NORMA   No problem.

MIMI   No, really... I really thought I broke it, so... thanks.

               There is a silence.

               About last night... I should have stayed. *(pause)* We've been surrounded by people and flowers and... paper plates for so long. *(pause)* I just.... It's a hard time.

NORMA   *(pause)* It's okay. *(pause)* Oh! I have something to show you. *(She rifles through the box she brought in.)* My goodness. Your mommy kept a lot of things.

MIMI   What are you doing?

NORMA   It's from your mom's closet.

MIMI   Okay...

NORMA   Your dad asked me to help...

MIMI   Yes, of course. What is all of this?

NORMA   Not sure if you want to keep anything...

MIMI   Did you want something? You can have it if you want.

NORMA   No, no. There's something here I thought you should have. *(She picks up the Singkil fans and hands them to MIMI. MIMI doesn't take them.)*

MIMI   *(deadpan)* What are those?

NORMA   These were your mommy's Singkil fans. *(She twirls them before presenting them to MIMI again.)* Here. They're yours now.

Mimi suddenly turns away from Norma. She is pinching her lip.

MIMI   There's something in my... I don't really need the fans. It's okay.

NORMA   You can just take them home with you.

Mimi turns around again, her face controlled again.

MIMI   What for?

NORMA   Just to keep. You can take this and the Sari Manok home and put them in a box somewhere. *(pause)* You don't even have to look at them. *(pause)* You just have to take them. *(pause)* They're yours now.

MIMI   *(fingering the beading on the fans, but still not taking them)* They're very pretty.

NORMA   Yes.

MIMI   Do you still have your fans?

NORMA   Yes, of course. I still teach every now and then.

MIMI   Good for you. My mother stopped dancing once she had a family.

NORMA   Well... you make decisions.

MIMI   What if she kept on dancing?

NORMA   But she didn't.

MIMI   But what if she did?

NORMA   Then maybe she would have been like me. I'm fifty-six and I don't have a nice daughter like you.

MIMI   I didn't mean to...

NORMA   Please. Keep these safe... they're yours now.

             NORMA hands MIMI the fans and she reluctantly takes them. NORMA exits.

             MIMI handles the fans, and after a moment starts to dance with them, clumsily.

act one
scene eleven

Lights change. MIMI's apartment. CHASE enters with shopping bags and finds her dancing with the fans.

CHASE   Hello, what's this?

MIMI   They were my mom's fans.

> *He looks clueless.*

They go with the chicken headdress.

CHASE   Oh.

MIMI   Stop looking at me.

CHASE   I can't. You look beautiful.

MIMI   What?

CHASE   You look so beautiful doing that fan thing.

MIMI   Thanks.

> *She stops dancing.*

CHASE   Don't stop. Really. You look beautiful.

> *CHASE tries to kiss her and she shies away.*

Are you still angry at me?

MIMI   No. Are you?

CHASE	Raving mad.
	Tentatively, he gently kisses her cheek, and she melts for a second. She eventually pulls away.
MIMI	What's all of this?
CHASE	I bought some groceries. See, I told you I contribute.
MIMI	You are silly.
CHASE	Oh! And you know who I ran into today?
MIMI	Who?
CHASE	Heidi from Dot Com. She wanted to let you know that everyone is thinking of you.
MIMI	No, she's wondering when I can start work again. That's what she was saying.
CHASE	No, I don't think it was that. I think she was worried. *(He brushes it off.)* Anywho... I got some ice cream—don't worry it's chocolate mint—and I also replenished our bread supply...
MIMI	I hate that place.
CHASE	You can always tell them you're not available...
MIMI	I don't want to go back.
CHASE	Then don't go back.
MIMI	And do what?
CHASE	What you want.
MIMI	That's easier said than done. You know how shitty that looks on a resume? I haven't stayed anywhere for more than a couple of years.

CHASE	That's not true.
MIMI	Dot Com. Vision Communications. Century Design.
CHASE	And before that?
MIMI	I was in college, Chase.
CHASE	Well that's *three* years of your life.
MIMI	No. I fast-tracked so that I could get the hell out of there.
CHASE	You can make money doing what you want, you know.
MIMI	Oh really? Like a fair amount of money ? To live comfortably? People need to work for a living.
CHASE	What's that supposed to mean?
MIMI	Novels don't pay.
CHASE	*(pause)* Thanks a lot.
MIMI	I'm sorry.
CHASE	No. I know you're just saying that to hurt my feelings.
MIMI	I'm sorry.
CHASE	Yeah. *(pause)* Why don't you take your time going back to work? I mean, you're mom just died.
MIMI	For fuck sakes, Chase, it's not about my mom!
CHASE	Hey, relax.
MIMI	Chase, I don't know what I'm doing.
CHASE	What do you mean?

MIMI	Life isn't as easy for me as it is for you. Look at you.
CHASE	That's not fair.
MIMI	No, really, Chase. You are one big fucking smile. All the time. You are a ball of positive energy. And I'm just a black hole. There's nothing inside me. I can't feel anything. And if I can't feel anything, what can I say?
CHASE	Are you kidding me? I work a joe job so that I have money to do what I want to do. You work a high-paying joe job so that you can run away from things. I'm happy, you're sad. Why? It's because your mom is dead.
MIMI	*(pause)* I have to go.
CHASE	Don't go. Sorry.
MIMI	I have to.
CHASE	Don't do that.
MIMI	I have to go.
CHASE	Go where?
MIMI	I don't know.
CHASE	Then stay.
MIMI	No. Please.
CHASE	No. No. I need you to stay right here and say what is on your mind. You're always rushing out and I'm always begging you to stay. I need you to talk to me. Now.
MIMI	If I could talk to you and tell you what I am feeling then I would. I stand in the shower every morning wondering what I am feeling and I can't even find the words to explain how this feels.

CHASE	Then say that.
MIMI	I don't want to! I don't want to tell you that I'm not happy! I don't want to tell you that I cry in the shower! I don't want to tell you that I hate my mother! *(pause)* I don't have anything to say. *(pause)* I have to go.
CHASE	No. No! Mimi! Mimi! *(He catches her by the arm.)* Listen, okay? It's not your fault. You know? It's not your fault she died.

They look at each other for what seems like centuries.

MIMI	Let me go.

He obliges and watches her leave.

act one
scene twelve

*The streets of Toronto. M*IMI *is running until she is stifled by the voice of her mother.*

*Flashback to Toronto, 1979, Knob Hill Farms grocery store. M*ARIA *enters with grocery bags in hand.*

MARIA   Mimi! Stop right there! Where do you think you're going?

MIMI   I need to go pee. *(She dances in pain.)*

MARIA   Not now.

MIMI   Mom!

MARIA   Will you stop it!

*M*IMI *stops complaining as she watches a man entering with his back to the audience.*

MAN   Hey.

MARIA   You found me.

MIMI   Who's that?

MARIA   *(to M*IMI*)* Mimi, enough! *(To M*AN*, giving him a watch.)* Here, take it. You keep on forgetting this. You're going to get me into trouble, you know. *(She moves to exit.)*

MAN   *(grabbing her arm)* When will I see you next?

MARIA   Not now...

ᴀɴ	Call me.
Mᴀʀɪᴀ	I will. *(She smiles. The Mᴀɴ reaches to kiss her.)*
Mɪᴍɪ	*(pees her pants)* Moooooom!
Mᴀʀɪᴀ	*(She sees the puddle at Mɪᴍɪ's feet.)* Shit!

> *Lights change. A deserted street, present-day Toronto. The sound of a cellphone ring. Mɪᴍɪ answers it, still shaken.*

Mɪᴍɪ	Hello? Yes. I'm… I just went for a walk. I need to just… clear my head. Chase, please! I'm not… feeling very good—

> *Lights change. Mᴀʀɪᴀ appears again, the Mᴀɴ holding her hand.*

Mᴀʀɪᴀ	Mimi! Stop right there!
Mᴀɴ	Where do you think you're going?

> *Mɪᴍɪ drops her phone. Screams.*

Mɪᴍɪ	Get away from me! Please!
Mᴀʀɪᴀ	You found us.
Mɪᴍɪ	Go away!
Mᴀɴ	When will you see us next?
Mɪᴍɪ	Go away!

> *Mɪᴍɪ moves to exit, but is intercepted by another Mᴀʀɪᴀ and Mᴀɴ. She screams.*

Mᴀʀɪᴀ	Listen, Mimi.
Mɪᴍɪ	Please!

MARIA   Listen.

           *Lights change. MIMI begins running about the stage, then
           faces forward, out of breath.*

MIMI   Mom. Mom! Your spirit is catching up to me, Mom. You
           think you can catch me, but you can't. I can't let you beat me.
           I'm going to keep on running. Run until I can't feel my legs
           anymore. I'm going to run just like you. Into the darkness.
           The way you ran from us. The day you chose him. I'm running
           and I can't stop. I'm running and you can't catch me, Mom.
           Mom! Mom! Get out of my life! Mom!

           *MIMI runs into the mess of bamboo, and the stage is
           transformed into a club. Music is blaring and bass-
           heavy as she makes her way past clubbers—all looking
           like MARIA and MAN. They move in slow motion as MIMI
           drunkenly collides into some of them; dances with others.
           A flash of light reveals a man who looks like CHASE in the
           crowd of MARIA/MAN groupings. MIMI dreamily heads
           his way. A flash of light. It's just another clubber.*

           Hello. What's your name? That doesn't sound like your real
           name. You look like a… Steven. I said you look like a Steven!
           You're a Steven, aren't you? I know! I know you're lying to
           me. No, I don't have a boyfriend. My name? I'm Mimi. I said,
           Mimi! I'm the daughter of a princess. *(She laughs heartily and
           the laugh becomes a weak cry.)* I'm sorry. I… I didn't mean
           to cry…*(She stops crying.)* Steven… can you make me feel
           better?

           Fade to black.

act two
scene one

The cast except for MIMI enters singing a ghostly chant. NORMA leads the way, moving and dancing in pseudo-tribal movements. Ceremoniously, NESTOR carries a very weak MARIA in his arms. NESTOR places her centre stage and the group starts to dance about her, slowly and solemnly. With what little strength MARIA has, she sits up and tries to speak.

MARIA   Mimi.... Listen, Mimi...

NESTOR approaches MARIA's body with dagger in hand.

NESTOR   You betrayed me!

NESTOR stabs MARIA in the stomach and MARIA lets loose a horrid cry.

Blackout. Lights up on MIMI in her bed getting up with a start after a bad nightmare. CHASE enters and without looking at her, gathers his things.

MIMI   Chase?

CHASE continues to pack. MIMI watches him silently. CHASE heads towards the door.

Chase? Where are you going?

CHASE gives her a man's watch.

I can explain... *(She stops short of explaining herself.)*

Lights change. Flashback to the Perez apartment, 1979.

Whose watch is this, Mommy?

Lights up on MARIA, getting dressed, not looking at MIMI.

MARIA   It's... it's my friend's watch.

MIMI   It's like Daddy's watch.

MARIA   *(long pause)* I.... Listen, *anak*, I'm going out tonight. You stay here with your dad, okay?

MIMI   You're going to see your friend?

MARIA   *(pause)* Yes.

MIMI   To give him back his watch?

MARIA   *(pause)* Yes.

MIMI   What's your friend's name?

MARIA   No more questions, Mimi.

MIMI   Why?

MARIA   Give me that watch.

MIMI   But I want to see if this watch fits Daddy.

MARIA   No! *(She calms herself down.)* No, baby, I have to leave now. *(She tries to take it away from MIMI.)*

MIMI   Mom! *(MIMI pulls the watch right back with all her strength.)* I want to show this to Daddy!

MARIA   Mimi!

MARIA slaps her. Pause.

Mimi, darling.

MIMI runs away.

Lights change. The MAN is sitting with his back to the audience, smoking a cigarette. He puts on his watch.

MAN   You look beautiful.

MARIA   What?

MAN   You look beautiful doing that fan thing.

MARIA looks down, ashamed.

Pick them up.

MARIA obliges.

Dance for me. Go on.

MARIA obliges. She dances with her heart into it at first, but begins to feel foolish in front of him.

What is it?

MARIA   This is not right.

MAN   Dancing?

MARIA   No. This.

MAN   Jesus.

MARIA   I'm sorry.

MAN   Stop.

MARIA   I'm not having fun anymore.

MAN   Fine.

MARIA   I'm sorry.

           Lights down on MARIA, *lights up on* MIMI *and* CHASE.

MIMI   I'm sorry.

           CHASE kisses MIMI *on the forehead with finality. She grabs his arm but he eventually frees himself and exits.*

           An eerie chant is heard once again.

           Chase. Please don't leave.

           The chant begins to swell out of control.

act two
scene two

NORMA and NESTOR enter at opposite ends of the stage, slowly moving towards one another. NORMA is pursuing NESTOR, NESTOR is blindly moving about the bamboo.

NORMA   I will tell him face to face.

NESTOR   Follow the sounds. My hand patting the wall.

NORMA   Tell him what I told him on paper many years ago.

NESTOR   Go down the stairs. No one knows. No one notices.

NORMA   Now is the time. I will tell him everything I want to say.

NESTOR   No one knows but me.

NORMA   He must know. He must.

NESTOR   The colours, the shadows.

NORMA/NESTOR   I cannot make a mistake.

They collide into one another. Lights change. The Perez kitchen.

NESTOR   Maria?

NORMA   *(pause)* It's me, Norma.

NORMA looks away from him. With disappointment she begins to circle him, randomly placing bamboo poles about him like a cage.

NESTOR	I'm sorry. I'm... so sorry. *(He holds his head in his hands, stifling tears.)*
NORMA	Nestor?
NESTOR	Yes?
NORMA	You read the letter?

MARIA enters, she begins to encircle NESTOR as well, joining NORMA in caging him.

NESTOR	Yes. It was a long time ago.
NORMA	Does it matter? Should I have told you?
MARIA	Do I not matter?
NESTOR	Of course you matter...
MARIA/NORMA	Do you not care?
NESTOR	Of course I care...
MARIA	Then fight! Fight, Nestor!
NORMA	Why didn't you answer me?
NORMA/MARIA	I'm right here and you're letting me go.
NESTOR	I'll be a good father—
MARIA	Be a good husband!
NORMA	You were a good husband. Why, Nestor? What happened that you're still hanging on?
NESTOR	Please! Stay! I should have gone with you...
MARIA	I have to go.

NORMA   I can't stay forever, Nestor.

               *NORMA and MARIA exit. NESTOR continues to navigate his
               way about the bamboo cage blindly.*

NESTOR   Maria! Stay beside me! I know! I know I could have done
               better! I should have danced with you I should have danced
               and jumped and sang as loud as I could I should have yelled
               I should have been there I should have talked to you I should
               have I should have kissed you before you left that day I should
               have woken you up in the middle of the night to make love to
               you to show you it was me beside you smelling you not him
               to tell you that you were mine to tell you I loved you.

               I should have... Maria!

               *Lights change. Flashback to three months ago. NESTOR
               watches the past flash before his eyes. A spotlight on
               MARIA. She is putting her coat on, a hat and a scarf.
               MIMI can be seen in the distance watching TV.*

MARIA   Nestor? Mimi? I'm walking over to the store. Do you need
               anything?

MIMI   *(She doesn't turn her head to MARIA.)* Nothing.

NESTOR   *(watching as the present NESTOR)* Nothing.

MARIA   Nestor, do you want to come with me?

NESTOR   Later, *na lang.* I have to cook dinner.

MARIA   *Sige.*

               *She leaves the house and a set of headlights can be seen
               in the distance. The sound of tires screeching.*

               At the sound of the crash, NESTOR drops to the floor.

               The Perez house.

Nestor is sopping up water from the floor that came from a pot on the stove. Mimi enters at the sound of his fall.

MIMI   Dad! What's going on?

NESTOR   Nothing, nothing.

            Norma enters.

NORMA   What happened?!

MIMI   Dad... *(at the sight of his hand that seems to be burnt)* your hand. It's burnt.

NESTOR   It was an accident.

            He moves to the side and collides with Norma.

NORMA   Nestor. *(She cradles his face and looks into his eyes.)*

            Fade to black.

act two
scene three

An ER room. Lights up on MIMI *as she enters.* NESTOR
sits with his coat in hand on the examination table.
NORMA *stands near him.*

MIMI   *(She sits beside her father.)* I was talking to the doctor and
he said you'll need some help at home. I'll stay over tonight.
Before we go home, though, we should stop off at Shoppers
for a cane. The doctor says you'll need it to get around. Jeez.
I knew this was going to happen. *(takes out piece of paper and
pen)* Okay, let's make a list. Cane. The ointment for your hand.
Good news is you don't need to buy those silly sunglasses.
But we may have to consider proofing the house so that you
don't bump into things. I'll help you with that tonight.

NESTOR   I don't need help.

MIMI   Don't be silly.

NESTOR   Today was just an accident.

MIMI   You want this to happen again? Think, Dad. There's nothing
wrong with people helping you.

         Pause. NESTOR *gives a look to* NORMA.

NORMA   Mimi, maybe we should go.

MIMI   Not right now. *(to* NESTOR*)* Dad, we need to talk about this.

         NESTOR *is silent.*

Dad! Hello! Are you ignoring me now? Stop being a child.

Mimi tries to take his hands, but he breaks free, attempts to come off the examination table and stumbles onto the floor.

Dad!

She reaches down to help pick him up.

NESTOR   Get your... hands... off me!

NORMA   *Sige na, anak.*

MIMI   Stay out of this. Dad, give me your hand.

NESTOR   No! You think I don't know what I'm doing?! You think I can't take care of myself?!

MIMI   I never said that!

NESTOR   I know things. I...

MIMI   You don't know how to get around by yourself. Not yet.

NESTOR   I do know! I know everything!

Lights up on MARIA.

MARIA   I'm sorry.

NESTOR   I can't look at you.

MARIA   Please.

NORMA   Dear Nestor...

NESTOR   What did I do?

MARIA   You didn't do anything.

NORMA   *(frustrated)* Dear Nestor...

NESTOR	Did I do too little?
MARIA	Nestor, please forgive me.
NORMA	*(growing ever frustrated)* Dear Nestor...
NESTOR	You made me a fool. I would look at you straight into your eyes and wait.
MARIA	Nestor, please look at me.
NESTOR	And I would wait for you to tell me.
NORMA	Dear Nestor... Nestor... I write these words knowing you will never answer me.
MARIA	I couldn't. I was so ashamed.
NORMA	Dear Nestor. Dear Nestor. All my love. All my heart. Norma.

Lights change.

NESTOR	All of those years. I did it for you. I stayed for you.
MIMI	That is so unfair!
NESTOR	You wonder why I stuck around when I knew what was going on, when I could smell the scent of cigarettes and cologne on her neck? You would understand if you could look into the eyes of your child and see that she needs you. My only reward would be when I would climb into bed next to your mother. In the darkness, while she lay dreaming, I thought she was mine. But she never was.

Pause.

MIMI	Dad, I should have told you—
NESTOR	You knew.

MIMI	*(pause)* Everyone knew.
NESTOR	You must think I'm stupid.
MIMI	I never said that.
NESTOR	Staying all these years. When you knew.
MIMI	I never asked you. I never asked you to stay. So don't blame me when Mom never asked you to stay either.
NESTOR	Please leave.
MIMI	Don't do this.
NESTOR	Leave.
MIMI	But who's going to drive you home?
NESTOR	Give the keys to your *Ate* Norma.
MIMI	What?!
NESTOR	I want to be with someone who doesn't think I'm stupid.
MIMI	Don't put words in my mouth.
NESTOR	Leave.
MIMI	*(pause)* All right.

She gives her keys to NORMA *and exits.*

act two
scene four

Karaoke bar. A very drunk Mimi *picks herself up and finds a microphone on the floor. She looks for the mic switch. She finds it and turns it on. Feedback. She begins to sing. She takes a moment to sip her drink.*

KARAOKE CROWD MEMBER   Get off the stage!

          Mimi continues to sing.

          Get off the fucking stage!

MIMI   Shut up! I'm singing! *(She continues.)*

          Chase enters with Tammy *in tow.*

CHASE   Come on, Mimi.

MIMI   Chase!

CHASE   Come on…. We'll drive you home.

TAMMY   *(as though she is speaking to a deaf person)* Do you remember where you live?

CHASE   Tammy, she's drunk, she's not deaf.

MIMI   Fuck off, I'm singing.

TAMMY   Oh dear. Chase, I don't think she even knows who we are.

MIMI   What the fuck is she doing here?

TAMMY	Mimi, here, I learned this from St. John's Ambulance. Just put your arm over my shoulder and we can get you out of here.
MIMI	I can walk.
KARAOKE CROWD MEMBER	Then walk off the stage!
CHASE	Buddy! Can you wait a fucking minute! Come on, Mimi. Let's go.
MIMI	How did you know I was here?
CHASE	Come on, I'll give you a drive.
MIMI	You don't have a car.
CHASE	Tammy has a—
KARAOKE CROWD MEMBER	Get off the stage!
TAMMY	I'll start the car.

She exits.

CHASE drags MIMI off the stage. She leans on him, helpless.

MIMI	Wait! Where are we going? Is she? Is Tammy your…
CHASE	We're just hanging out.
MIMI	Why?
CHASE	Because… I'm just… doing things away from you. Please, Mimi. You're stepping on my foot.
MIMI	She's very nice.
CHASE	Yeah. She's very nice. Super nice. Tammy and I… are friends… right now… but you know what? It could turn into

something… so… I don't even know what the fuck I'm saying. *(pause)* Come on, we have to go.

MIMI   Just leave me here.

CHASE   What?

MIMI   Go ahead and be with Tammy.

CHASE   I don't have time for this—

MIMI   Go ahead and… *(MIMI weakly pukes on CHASE's shoes.)* Oh God. Oh God. I'm sorry. It's just… I miss you.

CHASE   I have to go.

    He begins to exit. MIMI catches up to him.

MIMI   Chase! Wait!

    CHASE turns around and its MARIA, with a skull for a face. Her hair begins to seep down to the floor and towards MIMI's feet. MIMI screams and exits.

act two
scene five

*Lights change. The Perez house. M*IMI *hysterically bangs on the front door.*

MIMI   Dad! Dad! *(She turns to the sound of the chanting.)* Stay away from me!

        *The chanting stops abruptly as N*ORMA *opens the door in her pyjamas.*

NORMA   What is it?

MIMI   There's someone behind me! Let me in! Let me in!

        *N*ORMA *looks outside and calmly closes the door.*

NORMA   *(pause) Anak*, there's nobody there.

MIMI   Can you not hear the voices?

NORMA   *Anak*... I can't hear anything.

        *M*IMI *listens for herself and hears nothing.*

MIMI   I'm sorry.

NORMA   What are you doing here so late, *anak*?

MIMI   I need to talk to my dad.

NORMA   He's still asleep.

MIMI   I need to talk to him, where is he?

NORMA	I just told you, he's sleeping.
MIMI	No really, I need—
NORMA	I heard you, *anak*, and I told you, he's sleeping. You can't wake him.
MIMI	Did he... why won't you let me speak to him?
NORMA	He can't talk right now. You have to leave him be. *Sige na...*
MIMI	Did he ask you to... *(calls upstairs)* Dad!
NORMA	Mimi! He doesn't want to speak with you right now!
MIMI	Who the fuck do you think you are? Walking in here, staying in this house...
NORMA	Don't get angry with me. Your dad just wants to be left alone.
MIMI	If you were here to pay respects to my mom, why weren't you at the funeral?
NORMA	*Aba!*
MIMI	Who are you really here for?
NORMA	Your daddy was my friend, too.
MIMI	I bet he was. Where is he? *(MIMI moves to exit.)*
NORMA	Go ahead. Find him. He won't wanna talk to you. That's what he told me.
MIMI	*(MIMI returns to NORMA, practically spitting in her face.)* Yes, I'm sure you're the expert on what my father wants and who my mother was.
NORMA	We were very close!

MIMI	Bullshit! You come here and speak about Mom like she was this wonderful person. That's not the person I knew.
NORMA	Mimi...
MIMI	She hated every minute I was alive. There was this wall around her. God forbid if we tried to climb over. God forbid if we tried to reach her on the other side!
NORMA	You calm down, *anak*!
MIMI	Fuck you!
NORMA	You want to know why your mommy chose family? You want to know why she chose you over dance?
	Lights up on MARIA.
MARIA	Norma... Norma, please don't cry. Take my hands. I want you to promise me that you will be happy.
NORMA	I can't promise you that.
	You have to stay!
MARIA	I have to go! *(pause)* Norma, I'm pregnant already.
NORMA	Is it Nestor's?
MARIA	Yes, of course!
NORMA	Does Nestor know?
MARIA	Not yet. Stop, Norma. Please.
NORMA	*(pause)* He loves you very much.
MARIA	I... I know that. I know.
NORMA	He is such a good man.

MARIA   Yes. He is.

NORMA   *(pause)* Please don't hurt him.

MARIA   What?

NORMA   *(pause)* You're... making a mistake.

MARIA   Norma!

NORMA   *(pause)* You are going to be lonely.

        Lights change.

MIMI   You were right. I was a mistake once I was born. *(She bursts into tears.)* That's why she hated me.

NORMA   No. Every woman can make a decision for themselves, Mimi. Your mommy made hers. But decisions are made with the help of fate. We don't make decisions without a guiding hand.

MIMI   You think a "guiding hand" led her to hate her life here? To hate us? To hate me?

NORMA   You think she hated you? *(She begins to rifle through her belongings and finds a newspaper clipping.)* Look!

MIMI   What is this?

NORMA   It's your mom.

MIMI   She's dancing the Singkil. Who cares?

        MIMI moves to exit. NORMA blocks her way, holding the picture right up to MIMI's face.

NORMA   Look at the date!

        MIMI looks at the back of the clipping.

MIMI   1974.

NORMA   She was pregnant with you. She was performing for the Philippine Consulate here in Toronto. All the newspapers published her photo back home. Her very last dance. That's what I meant when I said you have been dancing the Singkil your entire life.

MIMI   Please stop.

NORMA   No, you stop. Your mother is calling out to you.

MIMI   This is such bullshit.

NORMA   I think your mother has something to say, and you have to listen to find out what that is.

MIMI   This is ridiculous, *Ate* Norma.

NORMA   Do you know the story of the Singkil princess?

MIMI   What? Well, no. I told you already. I saw pictures. That was it. Why the fuck should I care?

NORMA   Because. Most people think it's about a Muslim princess who gets caught in the middle of an earthquake and her betrothed prince saves her. That's the story your mom knew. Here, alone in Canada. Making it through hard times, waiting. Waiting to be happy. When everything to make her happy was right in front of her.

MIMI   What's your fucking point?!

NORMA   Your mom was wrong. I was wrong. I was waiting, too. There is no prince. That's just the theatrical version. The prince was added for drama. The real story is of a princess that saves herself.

> NORMA *touches* MIMI's *forehead, and at the touch,* MIMI *embraces* NORMA, *starved for love. Lights change.*

*A Muslim chant is heard. M*IMI *watches as* N*ORMA leaves her embrace and joins the rest of the cast as they slowly take the tangles of bamboo and reconfigure them to look like a forest.*

act two
scene six

Lights change. The shadow of the headstone looms over
Mᴵᴹᴵ and the forest.

Mᴵᴹᴵ, with bouquet of flowers in hand, walks slowly
towards the headstone.

Mᴵᴹᴵ   Nice place you've got here. *(pause)* I bought you some flowers.
I don't know... you can just... *(She places the flowers atop the*
headstone. Pause.) Ate Norma said you liked Petula Clark. I
never knew that about you. I never knew my mother had
such bad taste in music.

      She laughs. She suddenly turns her back upstage.
      Breathing heavy, pinching her lips.

(under her breath) I can do this. Okay.

      She turns back to the headstone, taking it all in slowly.

I didn't mean what I said the other day when I said that I
hated you. I feel you over my shoulder every waking minute
since you died.

I remember walking down this long hallway at the hospital.
I knew. I knew even before the doctor told us that you were
gone. I could already feel you walking beside me.

The doctor told us that you didn't make it. As if you tried
to hang on. I couldn't believe that. I imagined once the
opportunity came, you let go. You gave in to the pull.

But I know now that can't be true. Not when you're everywhere.

Not when you can't leave me alone. Well, you... you don't have to worry anymore. I know you have something to say, and I'm trying to listen. I'll let you say it as much as you want for as long as it takes for you to say it. And if it's what I think you have to say, then my answer is, I'm going to forgive you.

Did you hear that, Mom? I'm going to forgive you now. I'm going to take everything that stings, that throbs and hurts inside my heart, and let it go. I'm going to forgive and be happy. *(pause)*

And if that's not what you want from me, then tough shit. I'll forgive you anyway. *(pause)*

When people ask me who my mother was, I will tell them she was a princess. A true princess. And I love her.

> *Mimi exits.*

act two
scene seven

Outside the Perez house. The bamboo forest wavers in the wind. A sunset is seen, the sound of wind blowing through trees is heard.

NESTOR sits on a log, facing away from the audience. MIMI walks towards him.

NESTOR   The sun is setting.

MIMI   Yes.

NESTOR   And I can't see it.

MIMI   I'm sorry, Dad.

NESTOR   No, I'm sorry. I'm sorry I never looked at more sunsets before. How does this one look?

MIMI   Like it's never going to end. Like it will never stay. *(She sits beside him. Pause.)* I never thought you were stupid.

NESTOR   I feel stupid sometimes.

MIMI   You're not. And I don't think it's stupid to accept help, either. *(pause)* I was thinking how strange it would be for you to get some weird nurse to help you with things. She wouldn't know what to cook, she wouldn't know what you like. I could help you out, you know. I could move in myself.

NESTOR   Are you sure?

MIMI   Pretty sure.

There is a long, thoughtful pause.

NESTOR   It would be nice.

MIMI   I know! I'll gain a ton of weight, but it'll be great.

NESTOR   It's not a good idea.

MIMI   What?

NESTOR   You need to do things for yourself now. I'll be fine. *(He lovingly taps her knee.)* This is my little girl.

MIMI   Can you at least let me cook for you?

NESTOR   You? Cook for me?

MIMI   Okay, okay. I'll help cook. Okay?

NESTOR   *(pause)* Okay.

> *They both laugh. A release. She holds his hand and looks at him.*

MIMI   What about *Ate* Norma?

NESTOR   To cook?

MIMI   To stay. *(He suddenly withdraws a bit, pensive.)* What? I don't know. I just thought you guys are friends already. *(pause)* Why don't you ask her?

> *NESTOR still looks pensive.*

What is it?

NESTOR   I loved your mom, you know?

MIMI   Of course you did.

NESTOR   I never wanted to hurt her.

MIMI   I know you didn't. And she didn't mean to hurt us, either.

NESTOR   That's why I have to find it in my heart to forgive her.

MIMI   Do you think that will ever happen?

NESTOR   Yes. I have to try. For me. *(pause)* Do you remember when we went to Wasaga Beach?

MIMI   Sort of.

> *The glow from a campfire is seen. NESTOR begins to stick a poker into the fire to toast marshmallows. The sound of nostalgic guitar music.*

NESTOR   Don't you remember? You must have been four or five. We tried to go camping.

MIMI   Oh my God! Yes! I remember. The KOA was disgusting... so many people with RVs. And we only had that stupid tent. I think we were the only brown folk in the camp. I wanted to go home immediately. You had a hard time starting the fire the first night, remember?

> *MARIA enters with hooded sweatshirt and shorts. NESTOR and MIMI watch her together.*

MARIA   *(at the sight of the fire)* You did it. You started the fire. *(She looks at NESTOR and smiles.)*

MIMI   Why the heck did we go camping?

NESTOR   To be together.

> *MARIA places her hand on NESTOR's. They watch the fire in silence.*

MIMI   But do you remember the bugs? Mom had to bring out this colossal can of bug repellant and she started spraying me with it. I could feel the sting in my eyes and I could taste it in my mouth. I didn't care, though. *(pause)* She rubbed it on me with such care. And then she let me sit in her lap all night. She zipped her sweatshirt around me so that I wouldn't be cold.

MARIA stands suddenly. Lights change.

MARIA   *(to MIMI)* Mimi! Stop right there! Where do you think you're going? *(MARIA's face changes.)* Come on. Sit down. *(MIMI sits.)* Sit closer! Ay, my God! *(MARIA takes out the bug spray.)* Okay, arms up. *(MIMI obliges and MARIA tickles her armpits.)* My fingers want to eat your armpits! Tickle, tickle, tickle! *(MIMI laughs and tries to crawl away.)* Hey! Come back here! *(She grabs MIMI by the legs and drags her closer. MARIA gives her belly a raspberry.)* Okay, legs up. *(MARIA rubs the repellant on MIMI's legs.)* All done. *(MIMI moves to exit.)* Hang on! Come here. Mommy has a secret for you. *(She whispers something into MIMI's ear. MIMI laughs.)*

NORMA enters. Lights change. MARIA drifts away.

act two
scene eight

*Mimi stands centre stage, facing the bamboo. Norma
ceremoniously hands Mimi her mother's fans. Drums are
heard as they begin to walk about the stage and speak in
a rhythmic fashion.*

NORMA   Ready, *ka na*?

MIMI   I am.

NORMA   Five, six, seven, eight, and...

Mimi strikes a pose with the fans.

Listen to your music. The music is guiding you. You guide the music.

MIMI   What do you mean?

NORMA   Do you know... Paula Abdul? *(Mimi nods, not knowing where this is going.)* You know how she choreographs, right? She listens to the music then she decides what dance movements go with the music.

MIMI   Yup.

NORMA   Well, in Filipino folk dance, we don't do that. See, I'll play this. *(The Kulintang plays a trembling hit.)* And you may begin to shake your fans in fear, right?

MIMI   *(This is getting more and more difficult.)* Okay.

NORMA   Then maybe I might see you do striking, staccato movements.

Then I might respond with this. *(The Kulintang plays a staccato strike.)* You see? We play off each other. When your mommy danced, you could never tell who was leading who. *(She sees Mimi's expression.)* Keep on going.

MIMI   Five, six, seven, eight, and...

> *Mimi strikes a pose with the fans.*

NORMA   Good. Head up, eyes down. Let your fans be an extension of your emotions. Five, six, seven, eight, and...

> *Mimi strikes a pose with the fans.*

Okay. Now, once you've improved on that, we can then move on to walking through the bamboo poles, gracefully.

> *The music stops abruptly.*

MIMI   Oh Jesus.

NORMA   Well, it is challenging, but that's what makes it exciting. There's so much danger.

MIMI   Danger?

NORMA   Oh yes! The bamboo poles never stop, they close when they close. And right behind you is your *Asik* girl.

MIMI   My what?

NORMA   She is like the lady in waiting. This was always played by me.

MIMI   Why didn't you ever play the princess?

> *Music resumes. Lights up on the scrim. An* Asik *dancer enters with umbrella in hand, dancing the* Asik.

NORMA   The *Asik* girl is a very important role. While the princess had to juggle her fan play with fancy footwork, I was always two steps behind, mirroring every movement. There were times where your mom would drop her fans in front of hundreds of spectators. And I was there, to pick them up. In true character, I handed them to her and bowed my head like the lowly slave girl I was. And your mom, in turn, would take them and wave her hand ungratefully. The crowd loved how we took our roles so seriously.

I don't think I would have ever taken the princess role, even if it were offered to me. I loved the sashay of my hips while I danced. And I loved watching your mom from a distance...

Lights up on MARIA.

MARIA   Norma, look, my hands are bleeding again!

NORMA   Your mommy and I used to put bandages on our fingers while we practised.

MARIA   I can always count on you.

MIMI   Bandages?

NORMA   Our fingers would bleed when we would practise our fan play.

MARIA   I'll miss you.

NORMA   I would always stop once my fingers would bleed. But your mommy would keep on going.

MARIA   Keep on dancing, Norma.

Lights out on MARIA. NORMA *thinks for a second and continues.*

NORMA   Okay... let's get back to work. Now imagine it: your prince enters.

Chase enters, looking at Mimi. Mimi is still, watching him expectantly. The lights change, with only Chase and Mimi seen as they encircle each other.

He looks at you, his princess. You've made it. You've survived.

MIMI   And what does he say?

NORMA   He is silent.

Chase moves to exit.

You need to stamp!

MIMI   Stomp?

NORMA   Take your right foot and stamp it. *(Mimi obliges in the fashion of a Singkil princess.)* Again. *(Mimi obliges.)* And again. *(Mimi stomps one last time and strikes a pose with her fans.)* You need him to stay. Tell him to stay. Show him.

Norma drifts offstage. Chase comes forward and trips over a bamboo pole.

MIMI   Oh God!

He limps about the stage, winded.

CHASE   Ewdsmfcjsd! Efnwrehf!

MIMI   Sit down!

CHASE   Frwfwef! Oh God! No, no. I'm fine.

MIMI   Are you sure?

CHASE   I said I was fucking fine.

MIMI	*(pause)* Okay.
CHASE	No, it's not okay.
MIMI	Fine.
CHASE	Fine. *(pause)* Can we just get this over with?
MIMI	Ummm…
CHASE	What now?
MIMI	I don't have your sweatshirt here.
CHASE	What? I… that's my favourite…. Where is it?
MIMI	I don't—
CHASE	You don't know?!
MIMI	No. I lied.
CHASE	You lied, eh? Big fucking surprise.
MIMI	I knew it would be the only way to get you to meet with me.
CHASE	This is fucking ridiculous.
MIMI	I called. I emailed you. What was I to do?
CHASE	Well I am not going to sit here and listen to you say sorry.
MIMI	I'm not.
CHASE	Because it's not worth my—what?
MIMI	I'm not going to say sorry.
CHASE	Well fuck you, too.

MIMI	No, listen. Can you look at me please?
CHASE	This is bullshit. You shut me out. You never would tell me what's on your mind. And now you want to talk.
MIMI	This time I have something to say!

CHASE moves to exit.

Do you remember the first time we met at Chapters? I knew when I saw you. I looked at you and I thought, this was it. You were it. And I better not fuck this up. But I did anyway. You gave and gave and gave, and I didn't give anything back. These last few weeks have taught me that. You leaving taught me that. So I didn't want to say sorry. I wanted to say thank you.

CHASE	You're welcome. *(He moves to exit again.)*
MIMI	I visited my mother's grave today. I did it. I said a lot of things to her. And I probably have a lot more to say. That's why I'll keep visiting her.
CHASE	I'm glad. *(He moves to exit.)*
MIMI	And I think if she met you she would have really loved you. Because I love you. *(CHASE looks away from her, deep in thought.)* Chase... I'm here. Jesus! I want to keep looking at you, right now. I never want to leave. I've been such a selfish person for such a long time. But there's a place here, inside of me now. No one else belongs there but you.

Pause.

CHASE	Please don't do this. I've walked through this moment a million times in my head before I got here just so that I wouldn't bend. I don't want to give in. I can't even look at you.

Lights up on NESTOR entering the Perez apartment bedroom, MARIA facing downstage, looking at her Sari Manok headdress. MARIA is too ashamed to look at him.

She tearfully places the headdress in a box.

Mɪᴍɪ approaches Cʜᴀsᴇ and offers her hands.

Mɪᴍɪ   I'm right here. *(She takes his hands and places them on her face.)* I'm right here. I'm not leaving.

Cʜᴀsᴇ   It's not that easy.

Mɪᴍɪ   I'm not asking you to make it easy for me. I'll prove it to you every day. And if you decide to leave anyway, then I'll accept that. But I'll still try to be a better person. Please give me a chance.

> *Nᴇsᴛᴏʀ places a hand on Mᴀʀɪᴀ's shoulder and at the touch, Mᴀʀɪᴀ melts into a soft sob. Nᴇsᴛᴏʀ cradles Mᴀʀɪᴀ in his arms and rocks her gently. Lights fade on Nᴇsᴛᴏʀ and Mᴀʀɪᴀ.*

> *Cʜᴀsᴇ is still looking away from Mɪᴍɪ as the lights fade.*

act two
scene nine

The lights change to symbolize the passing of days. The sun rises and sets, rises and sets. Lights up on MIMI sitting in full Singkil costume, staring at herself in the mirror. NORMA enters.

NORMA   You look beautiful.

MIMI   I think so, too.

NORMA   Do you need help with your bells?

MIMI   Please.

> *NORMA bends down to help tie MIMI's ankle bells on. She stops and looks into MIMI's eyes.*

Thank you, *Ate* Norma.

NORMA   I'm too old to be an *Ate*.

MIMI   Not to me.

NORMA   *(pause)* I think that's it.

MIMI   Thanks.

NORMA   Your welcome, *anak*.

MIMI   I mean it. Thank you.

NORMA   *(pause)* I hate to leave you guys.

Mimi looks at her long and hard through the mirror.

Mimi? Are you all right?

MIMI   I don't want you to leave.

NORMA   But I can't just—

MIMI   Talk to Dad.

Mimi embraces Norma.

Talk to him. I think he has something to say.

> *There is a knock at the door. CHASE enters. A look between MIMI and CHASE, NORMA leaves. CHASE looks at MIMI long and hard, poker-faced. After a pregnant pause, he smiles.*

CHASE   Hey, princess. Here are your fans.

MIMI   Thanks so much. Is everything set up out there?

CHASE   Yup. But are you ready?

MIMI   I am.

CHASE   You're stunning. *(He kisses her on the forehead.)* Shall I tell *Tita* Norma it's time?

MIMI   Yes.

act two
scene ten

The Perez house. NORMA and CHASE enter with NESTOR arm in arm. They sit him down.

NORMA   Okay, just sit tight.

NESTOR   I don't understand.

CHASE   It's a surprise, Mr. Perez.

NESTOR   Oh no.

CHASE   Hey—don't worry.

NESTOR   I am worrying.

CHASE   Just don't.

NESTOR   Mimi?

CHASE   She's not here.

NESTOR   Chase... please tell me. It isn't a stripper is it?

CHASE   No. No it isn't.

NORMA   Chase, can you bring the "you-know-what" in?

CHASE   Sure thing, *Tita.*

CHASE exits.

NESTOR   Norma, what's going on?

NORMA   Just relax, hah?

> *NORMA looks at NESTOR and gives him a solemn, final kiss to his forehead. She steps away but NESTOR holds her hand for a moment. He kisses her hand, then whispers something in her ear. NORMA smiles, nods, and whisper "yes" into his ear, then moves away from him, relieved. She wipes away her tears at the sight of CHASE entering with two long bamboo poles. NORMA gestures to be quiet.*

> *They carefully and quietly begin the Singkil beat: one-two-three, clap, clap. MIMI enters in full traditional Singkil costume, wearing her mother's Sari Manok and using her mother's fans. The sound of MIMI's ankle bells awaken something inside NESTOR. He knows what is being shown to him. She begins the dance. The height of the dance is broken when, unbeknownst to everyone on stage except for NESTOR, MARIA enters and sits on a chair beside him. She holds his hand.*

NESTOR   She's beautiful, isn't she?

MARIA   Yes. I can see her.

> *The dance ends and the lights fade to black.*

> *The End*

Karen Ancheta, photo by Mark McNeilly

acknowledgements

Just like the dance of the Singkil, it took many to make this play happen.

Salamat...

To Nina Lee Aquino and fu-GEN Asian-Canadian Theatre for looking past the very first (awful) draft of this play and letting it grow. To Yvette Nolan for letting me dream real big, just for the price of nachos. To Nadine Villasin, Leon Aureus, David Yee, Karen Ancheta, Rose Cortez, and the production team for making my words come alive. To all the Mimis, Nestors, Marias, Chases, and Normas who helped me develop this work. To Ric Knowles for making simplicity beautiful. To Mark McNeilly for reading every draft. To Factory Theatre for giving my play a home. To all the holes in the sky (L, H, G, F, A) who made the idea of mourning so clear. To Ari for reading my play on a moonlit night.

photo by Mark McNeilly

As the daughter of Cecille Estioko Hernandez, a pioneer of Filipino Folk Arts education in Canada, Catherine Hernandez is dedicated to the development of the Filipino-Canadian artistic community. Her first play, *Singkil*, was produced by fu-GEN Asian-Canadian Theatre Company in association with Factory Theatre and garnered seven Dora nominations, including Best New Play, Independent Division. *Singkil* is part of the Scarborough Stories anthology of works, which tell the tales of Toronto's dodgier east side. She has worked in one capacity or another with Carlos Bulosan Theatre, Native Earth Performing Arts, Buddies in Bad Times Theatre, and numerous others. Her new plays, *Kilt Pins* and *Future Folk* with the Sulong Theatre Collective, are in development at Theatre Passe Muraille, where Catherine is the 08/09 playwright in residence. She is now writing *Coyote* alongside poet Emma Ari Beltrán with Alameda Theatre Company.